# Ignite Your Entrepreneurial Spirit:

*Unleashing Success in the Business World*

## ***Introduction:***

Welcome to the exciting world of business and entrepreneurship, where dreams are transformed into reality and innovative ideas shape the future. In "Ignite Your Entrepreneurial Spirit," we delve into the dynamic realm of entrepreneurship, offering aspiring and seasoned entrepreneurs alike the essential tools, insights, and strategies to thrive in the competitive business landscape. Get ready to unlock your potential, embrace calculated risks, and embark on a transformative journey towards building a successful and fulfilling business.

# TABLE OF CONTENT

20. The Future of Entrepreneurship

## Chapter 1:

The Entrepreneurial Mindset: Igniting the Fire Within

In the exhilarating journey of entrepreneurship, success begins with the right mindset—a mindset fueled by passion, purpose, and a hunger for growth. "The Entrepreneurial Mindset: Igniting the Fire Within," lays the foundation for your entrepreneurial adventure, emphasizing the pivotal role of mindset in achieving your goals and realizing your dreams.

1.  Unleashing your passion and purpose as an entrepreneur:
    - Discover the driving force behind your entrepreneurial aspirations.
    - Tap into your passions and align them with your business endeavors.

- Cultivate a deep sense of purpose that fuels your motivation and guides your decision-making.

2. Adopting a growth mindset and embracing failure as a stepping stone to success:
    - Embrace a growth-oriented perspective that sees challenges as opportunities for learning and improvement.
    - Embrace failure as a natural part of the entrepreneurial journey and leverage it as a catalyst for growth.
    - Cultivate resilience and develop the ability to bounce back stronger after setbacks.

3. Developing resilience, adaptability, and a relentless drive for continuous improvement:
    - Strengthen your resilience to overcome obstacles and navigate through uncertainty.

- Embrace adaptability and agility in the face of changing market dynamics.
- Cultivate a thirst for continuous learning and improvement, constantly refining your skills and knowledge.

The above serves as a powerful reminder that success in entrepreneurship is not solely determined by external factors but is rooted in the power of your mindset. By igniting the fire within and nurturing a mindset of passion, purpose, growth, and resilience, you lay a solid foundation for the journey ahead. It is this mindset that will guide your decision-making, fuel your perseverance, and empower you to overcome challenges and embrace success.

Throughout the book, we will continually revisit and reinforce these core principles, intertwining them with practical strategies and insights to help you build a thriving and fulfilling business.

Get ready to unleash the full power of your entrepreneurial mindset and embark on a transformative journey toward success and personal fulfillment. The possibilities are boundless when you cultivate the right mindset to ignite the fire within you.

## Chapter 2:

From Idea to Reality: The Art of Business Planning

In this chapter, "From Idea to Reality: The Art of Business Planning," we embark on a transformative journey that lays the groundwork for turning your entrepreneurial dreams into tangible, successful ventures. This chapter places significant emphasis on the pivotal process of business planning and equips you with the essential tools and strategies to navigate this crucial phase effectively.

1.    Nurturing and refining your business idea:

- Immerse yourself in a creative exploration of potential business ideas and concepts.
- Learn techniques to nurture and develop your ideas, allowing them to flourish into solid foundations for your venture.
- Gain insight into identifying unique selling points and differentiators that will set your business apart from competitors.

2.    Conducting market research and identifying target customers:

- Discover the power of market research in understanding industry dynamics, consumer behavior, and market trends.
- Learn how to effectively gather data, analyze market segments, and identify your target customers.

- Harness the invaluable insights gained from market research to tailor your products or services to meet customer needs and preferences.
3. Crafting a comprehensive business plan:
   - Understand the significance of a well-structured business plan as a roadmap for success.
   - Gain a deep understanding of the essential components of a business plan, including executive summary, company description, market analysis, organizational structure, product/service offering, marketing and sales strategies, financial projections, and more.
   - Learn how to effectively communicate your vision, strategies, and goals in a concise and compelling manner.

By placing emphasis from this chapter, we empower you to lay a solid foundation for your entrepreneurial journey. From nurturing and refining your business idea to conducting thorough market research and crafting a comprehensive business plan, you'll be equipped with the knowledge and tools needed to bring your ideas to life and pave the way for future success. Embrace the transformative power of business planning and watch your entrepreneurial dreams unfold into a thriving reality.

## Chapter 3:

Building a Solid Foundation: Legal, Financial, and Operational Considerations

Building a Solid Foundation: Legal, Financial, and Operational Considerations, we delve into the critical aspects of establishing a strong and sustainable business foundation. This chapter emphasizes the importance of addressing key legal, financial, and operational considerations to ensure the long-term success of your venture.

1. Understanding legal structures and compliance requirements:
   - Gain a comprehensive understanding of different legal structures available for businesses, such as sole proprietorship, partnership, corporation, and LLC.
   - Navigate through the legal requirements and regulations specific to your industry and location.
   - Learn how to protect your intellectual property rights, draft contracts, and handle legal agreements effectively.
2. Managing finances, budgeting, and securing funding:
   - Develop sound financial management practices to effectively track and control your business's financial health.

- Learn the art of budgeting, forecasting, and cash flow management to ensure financial stability.
- Explore various funding options, including bootstrapping, loans, investments, and grants, and understand the criteria and processes involved.

3. Establishing efficient operations, supply chains, and systems:
- Optimize your business operations by streamlining processes, enhancing productivity, and minimizing costs.
- Develop effective supply chain management strategies to ensure timely delivery of products or services.
- Implement robust systems and technologies to enhance operational efficiency, such as inventory management, customer relationship management (CRM), and project management tools.

We highlight the crucial elements that contribute to a solid business foundation. Understanding legal requirements, managing finances effectively, and establishing efficient operations are essential for long-term success and sustainability. By addressing these considerations early on, you'll be better equipped to navigate potential challenges, mitigate risks, and build a resilient business that can withstand the test of time. Take control of your business's legal, financial, and operational aspects, and lay the groundwork for a strong and prosperous future.

## FOOD FOR THOUGHT

We not only delve into the practical aspects of establishing a strong business foundation but also offer inspiring food for thought to fuel your entrepreneurial journey.

Remember, your business's legal structure and compliance requirements are not just formalities—they shape your operations and build trust. Embrace the opportunity to choose the structure that aligns with your vision and approach compliance as a chance to build credibility.

Financial management is more than numbers—it's the lifeblood of your business. Embrace financial literacy and take control of your financial destiny. Each decision shapes your venture's future.

Operational efficiency is about optimizing processes, enhancing productivity, and delivering value. Embrace the mindset of continuous improvement and collaboration, using your supply chain as a strategic advantage. As you navigate these considerations, remember that challenges are opportunities for growth. Embrace the transformative power of building a strong foundation, and let it support your dreams for years to come. Stay resilient, determined, and embrace the possibilities that lie ahead.

## Chapter 4:

The Power of Effective Marketing: Reaching and Engaging Your Target Audience

The Power of Effective Marketing: Reaching and Engaging Your Target

Audience, we delve into the exciting realm of marketing and explore strategies to effectively reach and engage your ideal customers. This chapter places significant emphasis on the pivotal role of marketing in driving business growth and provides you with the tools and insights to create impactful marketing campaigns.

1.  Understanding your target audience:
    - Dive deep into understanding the demographics, psychographics, and behaviors of your target audience.
    - Develop detailed buyer personas that capture the essence of your ideal customers.
    - Gain insights into their pain points, desires, and motivations, enabling you to tailor your marketing messages effectively.
2.  Crafting a compelling brand identity:

- Define your unique value proposition and establish a strong brand identity.
- Develop a captivating brand story that resonates with your target audience.
- Create a consistent and memorable visual identity through your logo, colors, typography, and overall brand aesthetics.

3. Implementing multi-channel marketing strategies:
- Explore a range of marketing channels, including digital platforms, social media, content marketing, email marketing, and traditional advertising.
- Develop an integrated marketing strategy that leverages the strengths of each channel to maximize reach and engagement.

- Use data analytics to track the effectiveness of your marketing efforts and refine your strategies based on insights.

4.    Building meaningful customer relationships:

- Embrace the power of building strong and authentic relationships with your customers.
- Engage with your audience through personalized communication, community-building initiatives, and exceptional customer service.
- Leverage customer feedback and insights to continuously improve your products, services, and overall customer experience.

We highlight the crucial role that effective marketing plays in driving business success. Understanding your target audience, crafting a compelling brand identity, implementing multi-channel marketing strategies, and building meaningful customer relationships are key pillars of successful marketing. By mastering these strategies, you'll be able to create impactful campaigns that resonate with your audience, drive brand awareness, and ultimately lead to business growth. Embrace the power of marketing and unlock the potential to connect with your customers in meaningful ways.

## Chapter 5:

The Art of Effective Leadership: Guiding Your Team to Success

The Art of Effective Leadership: Guiding Your Team to Success, we delve into the critical role of leadership in driving organizational growth and fostering a positive work culture. This chapter places significant emphasis on the essential skills and qualities needed to become an effective leader.

1.    Understanding leadership styles:
   - Explore various leadership styles, such as transformational, democratic, and servant leadership.
   - Gain insights into your own leadership strengths and areas for development.
   - Adapt your leadership approach to different situations and team dynamics.
2.    Communicating with clarity and purpose:
   - Develop strong communication skills to articulate your vision, goals, and expectations.

- Foster an environment of open and transparent communication, encouraging feedback and active listening.
- Inspire and motivate your team through effective storytelling and persuasive communication.

3. Building and nurturing high-performing teams:

- Understand the importance of team dynamics and diversity in driving innovation and productivity.
- Foster a culture of trust, collaboration, and mutual respect within your team.
- Provide opportunities for professional growth and development, empowering team members to reach their full potential.

4. Making strategic decisions:

- Develop strategic thinking skills to assess opportunities, risks, and challenges.
- Make informed decisions based on data, analysis, and intuition.
- Involve your team in the decision-making process to promote a sense of ownership and commitment.

5. Leading through change and adversity:

- Embrace change as an opportunity for growth and transformation.
- Guide your team through periods of change with empathy, clear communication, and support.
- Demonstrate resilience and adaptability in the face of adversity, inspiring your team to do the same.

Placing emphasis on the Chapter above, we highlight the crucial role of effective leadership in driving organizational success.

Understanding leadership styles, communicating with clarity, building high-performing teams, making strategic decisions, and leading through change and adversity are key aspects of effective leadership. By honing your leadership skills, you'll empower your team, foster a positive work culture, and guide your organization toward sustainable growth. Embrace the art of effective leadership and unlock the full potential of your team and business.

# Chapter 6:

Navigating Challenges and Overcoming Obstacles

Navigating Challenges and Overcoming Obstacles, we explore the inevitable hurdles and obstacles that arise on the entrepreneurial journey. This chapter places significant emphasis on equipping you with strategies and insights to effectively navigate challenges and emerge stronger on the path to success.

1. Embracing a mindset of resilience:
   - Understand that challenges are a natural part of the entrepreneurial journey.
   - Cultivate resilience, adaptability, and a positive outlook to overcome setbacks and bounce back stronger.
2. Developing problem-solving skills:

- Hone your problem-solving abilities to effectively tackle obstacles and find creative solutions.
- Embrace a proactive and analytical approach to identify root causes and develop strategies for resolution.

3. support and building a network:

- Recognize the value of a supportive network of mentors, peers, and advisors.
- Seek guidance, advice, and feedback from experienced individuals who can provide valuable insights and perspective.

4. Leveraging lessons learned from failures:

- Embrace failures as learning opportunities and extract valuable lessons from them.
- Analyze past experiences to identify areas for improvement and make informed decisions moving forward.

5.    Cultivating a growth mindset:
   - Adopt a growth-oriented mindset that views challenges as opportunities for growth and learning.
   - Continuously invest in personal and professional development to enhance your skills and knowledge.

We underscore the importance of navigating challenges and overcoming obstacles on the entrepreneurial journey. Embracing resilience, developing problem-solving skills, seeking support, leveraging lessons learned from failures, and cultivating a growth mindset are essential for surmounting hurdles and achieving success. By equipping yourself with these strategies and insights, you'll be better prepared to face challenges head-on and turn them into stepping stones toward your goals. Embrace the journey, learn from setbacks, and emerge stronger and more resilient on your path to entrepreneurial success.

# Chapter 7:

Growth Strategies and Scaling Your Business

Growth Strategies and Scaling Your Business, we delve into the exciting realm of expanding your business and taking it to new heights. This chapter places significant emphasis on the strategies and considerations involved in achieving sustainable growth and effectively scaling your operations.

1. Exploring different growth strategies:
   - Understand various growth strategies, such as market expansion, product diversification, strategic partnerships, and mergers/acquisitions.

- Evaluate the suitability of each strategy based on your business goals, industry dynamics, and market conditions.

2. Managing scalability and resource allocation:
   - Prepare your business for growth by ensuring scalability in operations, infrastructure, and systems.
   - Optimize resource allocation, including finances, human resources, and technology, to support increased demand and expansion.

3. Implementing effective marketing and sales strategies:
   - Develop targeted marketing campaigns to reach new customers and penetrate new markets.
   - Fine-tune your sales strategies to capitalize on growth opportunities and maximize revenue generation.

4.    Cultivating strategic alliances and partnerships:

- Identify potential strategic partners who can complement your business and help accelerate growth.
- Nurture strong relationships with suppliers, distributors, and other key stakeholders to leverage their expertise, resources, and networks.

5.    Monitoring and adapting to market trends:

- Stay abreast of market trends, customer preferences, and industry developments.
- Adapt your products, services, and strategies to align with evolving market demands and seize growth opportunities.

Exploring growth strategies, managing scalability, cultivating strategic alliances, implementing effective marketing and sales strategies, and monitoring market trends are key considerations for achieving sustainable growth.

By implementing these strategies thoughtfully and staying adaptable, you can position your business for success in a dynamic marketplace. Embrace the excitement of growth, seize opportunities, and navigate the challenges of scaling your business to unlock its full potential.

## Chapter 8:

Sustaining Success and Leaving a Lasting Legacy

Sustaining Success and Leaving a Lasting Legacy, we delve into the crucial aspects of maintaining long-term success and creating a meaningful impact through your business. This chapter places significant emphasis on strategies and considerations for sustaining growth, fostering sustainability, and leaving a positive legacy.

1.    Balancing success and fulfillment:
   - Define what success means to you beyond financial achievements.
   - Cultivate a sense of fulfillment by aligning your business with your values, purpose, and personal goals.
2.    Incorporating sustainability and social responsibility:
   - Embrace sustainable business practices that minimize environmental impact and promote social responsibility.
   - Integrate sustainability into your operations, supply chain, and product/service offerings.
3.    Nurturing a positive organizational culture:
   - Foster a supportive and inclusive work environment that values diversity, collaboration, and employee well-being.

- Encourage a culture of continuous learning, innovation, and personal growth.
4. Planning for long-term success and transition:
    - Develop a robust succession plan that ensures the continuity of your business beyond your leadership.
    - Prepare for future growth, changes, and potential exit strategies by aligning your business with market trends and customer needs.
5. Engaging in philanthropy and giving back:
    - Identify opportunities to contribute to your community and make a positive social impact through philanthropic initiatives.
    - Consider ways to leverage your resources, expertise, and influence to

support causes that align with your values.

Balancing success and fulfillment, incorporating sustainability and social responsibility, nurturing a positive organizational culture, planning for long-term success and transition, and engaging in philanthropy are essential considerations for creating a meaningful and enduring impact. By integrating these principles into your business practices, you can create a legacy that extends beyond financial success, leaving a positive mark on your industry, community, and the world. Embrace the opportunity to make a difference and build a business that stands the test of time, leaving a lasting legacy of success and significance.

# Chapter 9:

Embracing Innovation and Disruption:
Pioneering the Future

Embracing Innovation and Disruption:
Pioneering the Future, we embark on a thrilling

exploration of the power of innovation and disruption in shaping the business landscape. This chapter places significant emphasis on the mindset and strategies needed to embrace innovation and position yourself as a leader in driving change.

1.   Recognizing the importance of innovation:
     - Understand that innovation is not just a buzzword but a driving force behind sustainable growth and competitive advantage.
     - Embrace a mindset that values continuous improvement, curiosity, and a willingness to challenge the status quo.
2.   Identifying opportunities for disruption:
     - Keep a keen eye on emerging technologies, market trends, and changing customer needs that present opportunities for disruption.

- Seek out untapped markets, unmet customer demands, and outdated business models that can be disrupted for greater impact.
3. Cultivating a culture of creativity and experimentation:
    - Foster an environment that encourages and rewards creative thinking, experimentation, and calculated risk-taking.
    - Empower your team to explore new ideas, learn from failures, and adapt quickly to changing circumstances.
4. Embracing emerging technologies:
    - Stay informed about the latest technological advancements and their potential applications in your industry.
    - Embrace the opportunities offered by technologies such as artificial intelligence, block chain, Internet of

Things (I.O.T), and automation to drive innovation and efficiency.

5.    Navigating challenges and resistance:
- Anticipate challenges and potential resistance to change, both internally and externally.
- Develop strategies to overcome resistance, communicate the benefits of innovation, and build buy-in from stakeholders.

We underscore the significance of embracing innovation and disruption in shaping the future of your business. Recognizing the importance of innovation, identifying opportunities for disruption, cultivating a culture of creativity, embracing emerging technologies, and navigating challenges are key elements of pioneering the future. By staying at the forefront of innovation and embracing the opportunities presented by disruptive forces, you can position yourself as a trailblazer in your industry and lead the way toward a successful and impactful future. Embrace the power of innovation and disruption, and unleash your potential to shape the future of your business and the world around you.

**Chapter 10:**

# The Art of Networking and Building Relationships: Fueling Business Growth

The Art of Networking and Building Relationships: Fueling Business Growth, we delve into the invaluable power of networking and relationship-building in driving your business forward. This chapter places significant emphasis on the strategies and skills needed to cultivate meaningful connections and harness the potential of your professional network.

1. Understanding the importance of networking:
   - Recognize that networking is not just about making contacts but building mutually beneficial relationships.
   - Embrace the opportunities that networking presents for collaboration, partnerships, and business growth.
2. Building a strong personal brand:

- Define your unique value proposition and cultivate a compelling personal brand.
- Develop a clear and consistent message that resonates with your target audience and sets you apart from competitors.

3. Leveraging online and offline networking platforms:

- Utilize both online platforms, such as professional networking sites

# Chapter 11:

Harnessing Technology for Business Success

Harnessing Technology for Business Success, within the book "Ignite Entrepreneur Spirit," we delve into the transformative role of technology in driving business growth and achieving entrepreneurial success. This chapter places significant emphasis on strategies and considerations for effectively utilizing technology to fuel innovation, streamline operations, and propel your business forward.

1. Embracing digital transformation:
   - Recognize the need for digital transformation and the opportunities it presents for your business.
   - Embrace technology as a catalyst for innovation, efficiency, and competitive advantage.

2.    Identifying technology trends and opportunities:
- Stay informed about the latest technological advancements and their potential applications in your industry.
- Identify technology trends that align with your business goals and can offer a strategic advantage.

3.    Streamlining operations with automation:
- Evaluate your business processes and identify areas where automation can improve efficiency.
- Implement automation tools and systems to streamline repetitive tasks, reduce errors, and enhance productivity.

4.    Leveraging data analytics for informed decision-making:
- Harness the power of data analytics to gain valuable insights into your

customers, market trends, and business performance.

- Use data-driven decision-making to optimize strategies, improve customer experiences, and drive business growth.

Embracing digital transformation, identifying technology trends, streamlining operations with automation, leveraging data analytics, embracing e-commerce, enhancing cybersecurity, and adopting emerging technologies are key considerations for effectively harnessing technology. By leveraging technology strategically, you can gain a competitive edge, unlock new opportunities, and propel your business toward entrepreneurial success. Embrace the power of technology, adapt to the digital landscape, and harness its potential to drive innovation and business growth.

# Chapter 12:

The Entrepreneur's Journey: Self-Care and Work-Life Balance

The Entrepreneur's Journey: Self-Care and Work-Life Balance, we delve into the critical importance of prioritizing self-care and achieving a healthy work-life balance on the path to entrepreneurial success. This chapter places significant emphasis on strategies and considerations for nurturing your well-being while managing the demands of entrepreneurship.

1.    Recognizing the value of self-care:

- Understand that self-care is not a luxury but a necessity for your overall well-being and effectiveness as an entrepreneur.
- Embrace the concept of self-care as an investment in yourself and your business.

2. Prioritizing physical and mental health:
- Make time for regular exercise, healthy eating, and adequate rest to maintain physical well-being.
- Cultivate practices that support mental health, such as mindfulness, meditation, and stress management techniques.

3. Embracing leisure and rejuvenation:
- Incorporate leisure activities, hobbies, and downtime into your schedule to recharge and rejuvenate.
- Engage in activities that bring joy, relaxation, and fulfillment outside of work.

4. Cultivating a support network:
   - Build connections with fellow entrepreneurs, mentors, or like-minded individuals who understand the entrepreneurial journey.
   - Seek support and guidance from this network, share experiences, and learn from one another.
5. Reflecting on purpose and fulfillment:
   - Regularly reflect on your purpose and values to ensure alignment with your entrepreneurial endeavors.
   - Evaluate your business goals and activities to ensure they contribute to your overall fulfillment and well-being.

We underscore the vital role of self-care and work-life balance in the entrepreneurial journey. Recognizing the value of self-care, prioritizing physical and mental health, setting boundaries, delegating tasks, embracing leisure, cultivating a support network, and reflecting on purpose and fulfillment are key considerations for achieving a healthy work-life balance. By prioritizing your well-being, you can sustain your energy, creativity, and effectiveness as an entrepreneur, leading to long-term success and fulfillment. Embrace the journey, nurture yourself along the way, and create a harmonious balance between your entrepreneurial aspirations and personal well-being.

## Chapter 13:

The Power of Continuous Learning and Adaptation

We explore "The Power of Continuous Learning and Adaptation" in the entrepreneurial journey. This chapter emphasizes the transformative impact of ongoing learning and adaptability, providing practical strategies and a mindset shift to thrive in a rapidly changing business landscape.

1.    Embracing a Growth Mindset:
   - Cultivate a mindset that embraces learning and growth.
   - Embrace challenges as opportunities for personal and professional development.
   - View failures as valuable learning experiences and stepping stones to success.
2.    Seeking Knowledge and Staying Curious:
   - Foster a thirst for knowledge and actively seek learning opportunities.
   - Stay updated on industry trends, market shifts, and emerging technologies.
   - Engage in continuous learning to stay ahead of the competition.
3.    Pursuing Formal and Informal Learning:
   - Engage in formal education, workshops, courses, or certifications to acquire new skills and deepen expertise.

- Embrace informal learning through reading books, attending conferences, networking, and learning from mentors.
- Leverage online resources and educational platforms to access a wealth of information.

4.    Adapting to Change and Embracing Innovation:

- Stay agile and adaptable in response to market changes, technological advancements, and shifting customer needs.
- Embrace innovation as a driver of growth and explore new ideas, processes, and technologies.
- Continuously evaluate and refine your business strategies to stay relevant and competitive.

5.    Networking and Collaboration for Learning:

- Build a network of like-minded individuals, mentors, and industry experts.
- Engage in meaningful conversations, share insights, and learn from one another.
- Collaborate on projects or joint ventures to leverage collective expertise and drive innovation.

6. Embracing Feedback and Constructive Criticism:
   - Seek feedback from customers, peers, and mentors to gain valuable insights.
   - Embrace constructive criticism as an opportunity for growth and improvement.
   - Use feedback to refine products, services, and business strategies.

By emphasizing the power of continuous learning and adaptation, we equip entrepreneurs with the tools to thrive in a dynamic business environment. Embracing a growth mindset, seeking knowledge, pursuing formal and informal learning, adapting to change, networking for learning, reflecting on experiences, and embracing feedback are vital components of continuous growth and success. By adopting these strategies and cultivating a mindset of lifelong learning, entrepreneurs can stay ahead of the curve, innovate, and navigate the ever-evolving business landscape with confidence. Embrace the power of continuous learning and adaptation, and unlock your full potential as an entrepreneur.

## Chapter 14:

Leaving a Lasting Impact and Giving Back

By embracing social responsibility, defining your impact, incorporating sustainability practices, engaging in philanthropy, leveraging resources, measuring impact, and inspiring others, you can make a meaningful difference in the world. Your business has the potential to leave a legacy that extends far beyond financial success, creating positive change and contributing to a better future. Embrace the opportunity to make a lasting impact and leave a meaningful footprint on the world.

1.	Embracing Social Responsibility:
    - Elevate your perspective beyond business success and embrace a broader sense of purpose.
    - Recognize the power and responsibility you have as an entrepreneur to make a positive impact.
    - Embrace social responsibility as an essential part of your entrepreneurial journey.
2.	Defining Your Impact:
    - Reflect on your values, passions, and the legacy you want to leave behind.

- Identify the specific areas where your business can create a meaningful and lasting impact.
- Set clear goals and intentions to drive your efforts towards creating a better world.

3.    Sustainability Practices:

- Integrate sustainability into the core of your business practices and operations.
- Embrace environmentally conscious initiatives that reduce your ecological footprint.
- Inspire others by showcasing how sustainable practices can benefit both your business and the planet.

4.    Engaging in Philanthropy and Community Initiatives:

- Identify causes and organizations that align with your mission and values.

- Engage in philanthropic initiatives that have a direct and positive impact on your community.
- Encourage your employees and stakeholders to participate in volunteer activities and charitable giving.

5.  Leveraging Resources and Influence:

- Utilize your resources, networks, and influence to create significant change.
- Collaborate with like-minded businesses and organizations to amplify your impact.
- Pool resources and expertise to address societal challenges and drive collective action.

6.  Measuring and Evaluating Impact:

- Establish metrics and evaluation methods to measure the effectiveness of your efforts.

- Regularly assess the impact of your initiatives and adjust strategies as needed.
- Share the outcomes and lessons learned to inspire continuous improvement and transparency.

7. Inspiring Others to Make a Difference:

- Share your journey and experiences to inspire fellow entrepreneurs and individuals.
- Use your platform to educate and empower others to take action and make a positive impact.
- Encourage a collective effort towards creating a better future for all.

# Chapter 15:

# Effective Communication and Influential Leadership

By recognizing the power of effective communication, building rapport, crafting compelling messages, practicing active listening, nurturing emotional intelligence, leveraging communication for influence, and embracing continuous improvement, you can become a highly effective and influential leader. Your ability to communicate clearly, connect with others, and inspire action will empower your team, foster collaboration, and drive meaningful results. Embrace the art of communication, hone your leadership skills, and become an influential force in your organization and beyond.

1. The Power of Effective Communication:
   - Recognize that effective communication is the cornerstone of influential leadership.

- Understand the impact of clear and persuasive communication on building trust and inspiring others.
- Embrace communication as a tool to convey vision, values, and expectations.

2. Building Rapport and Connection;

- Cultivate strong interpersonal skills to establish rapport and connection with your team.
- Listen actively and empathetically to foster a sense of understanding and collaboration.
- Use effective verbal and nonverbal communication techniques to build positive relationships.

3. Crafting Compelling Messages:

- Develop the ability to articulate ideas and goals with clarity and conviction.
- Tailor your messages to resonate with different audiences and stakeholders.

- Use storytelling and compelling narratives to engage and inspire others.

4.     Active Listening and Feedback:

- Practice active listening to fully understand others' perspectives and concerns.
- Provide constructive feedback that promotes growth and development.
- Encourage open dialogue and create a safe space for communication and feedback.

5.     Emotional Intelligence in Leadership:

- Cultivate emotional intelligence to understand and manage your own emotions and those of others.
- Adapt your communication style to different personalities and emotional states.
- Use empathy and emotional awareness to connect and inspire your team.

6.    Influential Leadership through Communication:
    - Utilize communication as a tool to motivate, empower, and align your team.
    - Inspire others by sharing a compelling vision and values.
    - Lead by example, embodying the qualities and behaviors you want to see in your team.
7.    Continuous Improvement and Learning:
    - Recognize that effective communication and influential leadership are ongoing journeys.
    - Seek feedback and continually refine your communication skills.
    - Embrace opportunities for personal growth and development in communication and leadership.

# Chapter 16:

# Financial Management and Growth Strategies

Understanding the importance of financial management, developing a comprehensive financial plan, budgeting effectively, optimizing cash flow, considering financing options, exploring revenue generation strategies, and implementing risk management measures, you can drive sustainable growth and financial success. Embrace the power of strategic financial management, make informed decisions, and position your business for long-term prosperity and resilience.

1. The Importance of Financial Management:
   - Recognize the critical role of financial management in driving business success.
   - Understand the impact of effective financial planning and decision-making on long-term growth.

- Embrace financial management as a strategic tool for maximizing profitability and sustainability.

2. Developing a Financial Plan:

- Create a comprehensive financial plan that aligns with your business goals and objectives.
- Outline projected revenues, expenses, and cash flow to guide financial decision-making.
- Consider various scenarios and contingencies to ensure financial resilience.

3. Budgeting and Expense Management:

- Develop a budget that reflects your revenue projections and operational needs.
- Monitor and control expenses to optimize financial resources and minimize waste.

- Implement cost-saving measures and evaluate spending priorities.

4. Cash Flow Optimization:

- Manage cash flow effectively to maintain liquidity and meet financial obligations.
- Implement strategies to accelerate cash inflows and delay cash outflows when possible.
- Utilize cash flow forecasting to anticipate and navigate potential challenges.

5. Financing and Capital Structure:

- Evaluate different financing options and select the most suitable ones for your business.
- Assess the optimal capital structure to balance debt and equity.
- Regularly review and optimize your financing arrangements to support growth.

6.    Revenue Generation Strategies:
- Identify and explore opportunities to increase revenue streams.
- Evaluate pricing strategies, product/service mix, and market expansion opportunities.
- Developing strategies to enhance customer retention and foster long-term profitability.

7.    Risk Management and Contingency Planning:
- Mitigate financial risks through effective risk management strategies.
- Develop contingency plans to address unforeseen events or market fluctuations.
- Implement appropriate insurance coverage and establish emergency funds.

# Chapter 17:

Customer-Centric Approach and Brand Loyalty

By understanding your customers, delivering exceptional experiences, building a strong brand identity, cultivating loyalty, listening and responding to feedback, and continuously evolving to meet customer needs, you can create a loyal customer base that drives long-term success. Embrace the customer-centric mindset, prioritize customer satisfaction, and foster a strong emotional connection with your audience. By consistently delivering value and exceptional experiences, you can build brand loyalty that withstands competition and creates advocates for your business. Put your customers at the heart of your strategies and watch your business thrive.

1. The Value of a Customer-Centric Approach:
   - Recognize that a customer-centric approach is key to building a successful and sustainable business.
   - Understand the importance of placing the customer at the center of your strategies and decision-making.
   - Embrace a customer-focused mindset to create value, satisfaction, and loyalty.
2. Understanding Your Customers:
   - Conduct thorough market research to gain insights into your target audience.
   - Develop buyer personas to understand the needs, preferences, and pain points of your customers.
   - Use data analytics and customer feedback to continually refine your understanding of your customers.
3. Exceptional Customer Experiences:

- Design and deliver products and services that exceed customer expectations.
- Invest in personalized experiences, seamless interactions, and attentive customer service.
- Anticipate customer needs and proactively address their concerns to build trust and loyalty.

4.  Building a Strong Brand Identity:

- Define your brand identity and values to differentiate yourself in the market.
- Consistently communicate your brand message and values across all touch points.
- Foster an emotional connection with customers through compelling storytelling and brand experiences.

5.  Cultivating Brand Loyalty:

- Implement loyalty programs, rewards, and incentives to encourage repeat business.

- Establish strong relationships with customers through personalized communication and engagement.
- Create a community around your brand, fostering a sense of belonging and loyalty.

6. Listening and Responding to Customer Feedback:

- Actively seek customer feedback and listen to their suggestions, concerns, and feedback.
- Use customer insights to improve products, services, and overall customer experience.
- Respond promptly and effectively to customer inquiries and complaints.

# Chapter 18:

Globalization and International Expansion

Conducting market research, developing a strategic plan, adapting to cultural differences, navigating legal frameworks, building partnerships, and effectively managing operational challenges, you can expand your business into global markets. Embrace the potential of international expansion, seize opportunities for growth, and position your business as a global player. Successfully navigating globalization can lead to increased market share, diversified revenue streams, and a strengthened competitive position in the global marketplace. Embrace the challenge of international expansion and unlock the potential for global success.

1.   The Significance of Globalization:

- Recognize the impact of globalization on the business landscape.
- Understand the opportunities and challenges presented by global markets.
- Embrace globalization as a strategic avenue for growth and expansion.

2.  Market Research and Analysis:

- Conduct thorough market research to identify viable international markets.
- Analyze cultural, economic, legal, and political factors that influence market entry.
- Evaluate competitive landscapes and consumer behavior in target markets.

3.  Developing an International Expansion Strategy:

- Define clear objectives and goals for international expansion.
- Formulate a comprehensive strategy that aligns with your overall business vision.

- Consider market entry options such as exporting, licensing, franchising, or establishing local subsidiaries.
4.  Adapting to Cultural Differences:
    - Understand and respect cultural nuances in target markets.
    - Adapt products, services, and marketing strategies to cater to local preferences.
    - Foster cross-cultural communication and build relationships with local stakeholders.
5.  Navigating Legal and Regulatory Frameworks:
    - Familiarize yourself with international laws, regulations, and trade policies.
    - Seek legal counsel to ensure compliance with local requirements.
    - Mitigate legal risks and protect intellectual property rights during international expansion.
6.  Building Strategic Partnerships:

- Identify and collaborate with local partners, distributors, or agents.
- Leverage their knowledge, network, and expertise to facilitate market entry.
- Develop mutually beneficial partnerships to enhance brand presence and market penetration.

# Chapter 19:

Crisis Management and Resilience

Developing a crisis management plan, implementing effective communication strategies, making informed decisions, fostering resilience, learning from crises, and maintaining continuous preparedness, you can navigate through challenging times and emerge stronger.

Embrace crisis management as an opportunity to demonstrate leadership, build trust, and protect your business's reputation. By fostering a culture of resilience and adaptability, you can turn crises into catalysts for growth and development. Prepare your organization to face adversity head-on and emerge as a more resilient and successful business.

1. Understanding Crisis Management:
   - Recognize the importance of effective crisis management in maintaining business continuity.
   - Understand the different types of crises that can impact your business.
   - Embrace crisis management as a proactive strategy for mitigating risks and ensuring resilience.
2. Developing a Crisis Management Plan:
   - Create a comprehensive crisis management plan tailored to your business's unique risks and vulnerabilities.
   - Identify potential crisis scenarios and outline response protocols for each situation.
   - Establish a crisis management team and assign clear roles and responsibilities.
3. Communication and Stakeholder Engagement:

- Implement effective communication strategies to keep stakeholders informed during a crisis.
- Establish multiple communication channels to disseminate timely and accurate information.
- Engage with stakeholders proactively, addressing concerns and providing reassurance.

4.    Decision-Making under Pressure:

- Develop strategies for making informed and decisive decisions during a crisis.
- Anticipate and assess potential consequences of each decision.
- Remain adaptable and flexible in adjusting strategies as the crisis evolves.

5.    Resilience and Adaptability:

- Foster a culture of resilience within your organization.

- Encourage employees to embrace change and view challenges as opportunities for growth.
- Implement strategies to adapt quickly to changing circumstances and bounce back from adversity.

6. Learning from Crises:

- Conduct post-crisis evaluations to identify areas for improvement.
- Extract lessons learned and update crisis management protocols accordingly.
- Share knowledge and best practices across the organization to enhance preparedness.

7. Continuous Monitoring and Preparedness:

- Regularly assess and update your crisis management plan to reflect evolving risks.
- Stay informed about potential threats and emerging trends in your industry.

- Conduct regular drills and simulations to test the effectiveness of your crisis response.

# Chapter 20:

The Future of Entrepreneurship: Embracing Opportunities and Innovations

1. The Changing Landscape of Entrepreneurship:
   - Explore the dynamic shifts and emerging trends shaping the future of entrepreneurship.
   - Understand the impact of technological advancements, globalization, and societal changes.
   - Embrace the evolving landscape as a fertile ground for entrepreneurial opportunities.
2. Embracing Digital Transformation:

- Recognize the transformative power of digital technologies in reshaping business operations.
- Embrace digital transformation as a means to enhance efficiency, productivity, and customer experiences.
- Explore emerging technologies such as artificial intelligence, block chain, and the Internet of Things.

3. Sustainability and Social Impact:

- Embrace the growing importance of sustainability and social impact in entrepreneurship.
- Integrate sustainable practices into your business operations and supply chains.
- Seek opportunities to create positive social change while generating profit.

4. Entrepreneurship in the Gig Economy:

- Explore the rise of the gig economy and the opportunities it presents for entrepreneurial ventures.

- Embrace the flexibility and independence offered by the gig economy.
- Navigate the challenges and seize the advantages of this evolving work landscape.

In the final chapter of the book, we explore the future of entrepreneurship and the remarkable opportunities that lie ahead. By embracing digital transformation, sustainability, the gig economy, cultural diversity, lifelong learning, collaboration, and entrepreneurial leadership, you position yourself to thrive in a rapidly evolving world. The future of entrepreneurship is driven by innovation, adaptability, and a commitment to creating positive change. Seize the possibilities, embrace the challenges, and embark on a journey of entrepreneurial success in the dynamic landscape of tomorrow. The future is yours to shape, and with an entrepreneurial spirit, you can create a lasting impact and leave a legacy that inspires future generations of entrepreneurs. The future of entrepreneurship awaits—embrace it with open arms.